The Silurian Period: The History of the Prehistoric Era When Life Formed on Land

By Charles River Editors

A fossilised piece of Late Silurian sea floor

Amongst the fossils are fragments of the trilobite *Dalmanites*; the coral *Favosites*; bryozoans including *Favositella*; straight orthocone shells; brachiopods including *Atrypa*, *Leptæna* and a rhynchonellid.
Wenlock Epoch, Wenlock Limestone
Dudley, West Midlands

A picture of fossils dating to the Silurian Period

About Charles River Editors

Charles River Editors provides superior editing and original writing services across the digital publishing industry, with the expertise to create digital content for publishers across a vast range of subject matter. In addition to providing original digital content for third party publishers, we also republish civilization's greatest literary works, bringing them to new generations of readers via ebooks.

Introduction

A picture of fossils from the Silurian Period

The early history of Earth covers such vast stretches of time that years, centuries, and even millennia become virtually meaningless. Instead, paleontologists and scientists who study geochronology divide time into periods and eras.

The current view of science is that Earth is around 4.6 billion years old, and the first 4 billion years of its development are known as the Precambrian period. For the first billion years or so, there was no life in Earth, and then the first single-celled life-forms, early bacteria and algae, began to emerge. It's unclear where they came from or even if they originated on this planet at all, but this gradual development continued until around 4 billion years ago when suddenly (in geological terms) more complex forms of life began to emerge.

Scientists call this time of an explosion of new forms of life the Paleozoic Era, and it stretched from around 541-250 million years ago (Mya). In the oceans and then on land, new creatures and plants began to appear in bewildering variety, and by the end of this period, life on Earth had diversified into a myriad of complex forms that filled virtually every habitat and niche available in the seas and on the planet's only continent, Pangea.

One of the problems for those seeking to trace the history of life on Earth is that modern scholars are almost entirely dependent on fossil records, but the earliest types of life left few mongfossils. The best fossils are formed from the bones and hard body parts of dead creatures, but the earliest types of life were so small that they had no bones or cartilage and thus left no fossils. As a result, even though the Precambrian Period (4,600–541 Mya) covers over 80% of the entire history of the planet, scientists have very little idea of what forms of life existed then.

Although new species in the Cambrian explosion developed almost entirely in the oceans, the land was not entirely devoid of life. Though there were no plants or animals, mats of cyanobacteria and other types of microbes covered large terrestrial areas. Scientists have discovered the tracks of a creature that were left in mud that existed 551 Mya, and those tracks were left by leg-like appendages. Was this a fish-like creature that temporarily invaded the land, or was it something completely different than anything that exists today? There is no general consensus, but the Cambrian Period left a rich fossil record that provides a clear idea of the development of life during this time. At the same time, new discoveries are continually being made, and the more scientists discover about this mysterious period, the more their understanding of ancient Earth changes.

Following the Cambrian was the Ordovician Age, running from 445.4 million years ago to 444 million years ago. The shorter Silurian Age followed, a relatively stable and warm time from 443.8 million to 419.2 million years. The Devonian commenced in 419.2 million to 358.9 million, and was followed by the Carboniferous, Permian and Triassic Ages.

The Silurian Age occurred during the mid-Paleozoic, and despite its relative brevity, the era developed some interesting features that promulgated life on Earth. Roderick J. Murchison, a British geologist, named a sequence of rocks after a group of indigenous people called the Silures living in Wales during the mid-19th century. Despite their absence in the Silurian Age, the name was bestowed to honor the tribe.

Murchison was inspired by close friend Adam Sedgwick, who named the Cambrian Age, employing the Latin word for Wales. In 1835, the two presented a paper together entitled *On the Silurian and Cambrian Systems*. Their separate categorizing systems caused a serious enough disagreement over chronology that the friendship ended bitterly. The alternative name for Siluria was Gotlandia after the Baltica island of Gotland.

What ultimately precipitated these subdivisions in the chronology was a "famous unconformity"[1] on the River Onny in Shropshire. It indicated a natural break within "classic Silurian on its own home territory."[2] The timeline for beginning and end dates has remained imprecise, but the order of fossilized discoveries has proven correct. Joachim Barrande, a French paleontologist, geologist, and botanist, pursued the same issue in the Prague Basin of Bohemia. Studying the Paleozoic trilobite for a period of 10 years, his extensive work was published in his

---

[1] Britannica.com

[2] Britannica.com

Silurian System of Central Bohemia. Altogether, he identified and analyzed over 4,000 new fossil species, producing the enormous *Encyclopedia of Fossils*, numbering over 6,000 pages.

The Paleozoic

The modern understanding of the creation and development of planet Earth began to emerge in the early 19th century when geologists first began to analyze rock strata and to recognize that different layers contained different kinds of fossil remains. It was quickly realized that these provided a snapshot of life at various periods in the ancient past and it didn't take long before scientists began to use agreed terms to describe the vast stretches of time that comprise the history of our planet.

One of the first was a self-taught English geologist named John Phillips and in the 1830s he published a book that would change our understanding of the history of the planet and finally standardize the terminology used to describe these ancient periods. He did this by ordering rock strata according to the different types of fossils found within them and used this to define different periods of the development of life on Earth.

Phillips

These classifications describe the history of life after the Precambrian period in terms of three eras, with each being further subdivided into several periods. The Paleozoic Era (meaning the era of "ancient life") was the oldest and a period of dramatic upheaval and change. It covers a period from 550 million to 250 million years ago. This era began with the emergence of the first multicelled life and by its end, the first large reptiles, creatures such as Dimetrodon and Edaphosaurus, had appeared on the single continent, Pangea. This era is further subdivided into six geologic periods: Cambrian, Ordovician, Silurian, Devonian, Carboniferous and Permian.

The Paleozoic Era was generally a period of unbroken evolution of increasingly complex forms of life. However, it also included at least three of what have become known as "mass extinction events." For reasons that are not fully understood but are most likely associated with some form of climate change, there were three occasions during this era when many species completely died and were replaced by other forms of life.

The first of these events occurred between the Ordovician and Silurian periods. The Earth grew colder, glaciers appeared, and sea levels and sea temperatures dropped dramatically. Around 25% of all species on Earth were killed. In the oceans the effect was even more dramatic - around 60% of all marine species vanished forever.

At the end of the Devonian period there was a second and even more catastrophic extinction event that led to the death of around 70% of all species on Earth. Nobody is quite certain what caused this event, though current theories include excessive sedimentation of the oceans, a period of rapid global warming (or cooling), the impact of a comet or large meteorite, or even habitat changes caused by massive nutrient runoff from the land.

Then, at the end of the Permian period there was an extinction event so cataclysmic that it became known to early paleontologists as "the great dying." In a period that may have been a short as 20,000 years, 95% of all species of animal were wiped out and virtually all trees and many plants disappeared. Just like other extinction events, nobody is entirely sure what caused the great dying, but recent discoveries may give a strong clue.

Rocks in present-day Australia and Antarctica have been discovered that contain tiny quartz crystals marked with microscopic fractures. Quartz is incredibly strong and it would take enormous force to do this, many times the power of a nuclear explosion. It is thought that perhaps a huge asteroid more than three miles (4.8 kilometers) in diameter may have struck the Earth, causing a sudden and cataclysmic change in climate. Clouds of particles and gases would have blocked out the sun for months or perhaps even years. Global temperatures would have initially dropped, and corrosive rain and snow would have begun to fall. When this eventually stopped, the atmosphere would have been filled with greenhouse gases and a period of global warming would have followed that may have lasted for millions of years. Earth became a blank slate, ready for entirely new forms of life to appear.

The Blooming of the Silurian

The oldest estimation of the Silurian's commencement dates ranges from 445 million to 395 million years ago. Some believe that the period lasted no more than 18 million years, while others argue for close to 40. The marker for the Ordovician – Silurian boundary is not associated with any issue of climate change or any other physical phenomena. In 1885, the "golden spike"[3] or marker for the period's initiation is the emergence of the *Parakidograptus acuminatus*, a group of "concurrent *graptolite* species"[4] as the base for the Silurian System. The *graptolite* is an extinct marine invertebrate animal of the Paleozoic era forming mainly planktonic colonies.

The Silurian-Devonian border at the end of the age was published in 1977, and the turning point was fixed at the arrival of *Monograptus uniformis's* biozone, a single graptolite taxon (scientifically classified group or entity) "reinforced by associated conodont and trilobite taxa."[5] For many years, the Silurian was "simply a gap giving an unconformity in the geological sequence."[6] However, developments in the Silurian Age have come to be recognized as distinct and important to the future of Earth's evolution.

The Silurian Age is comprised of four sections. The first is Llandovery, named for a town in Carmarthenshire, Wales. Llandovery fossils are found in shale, sandstone, and gray mudstone sediment. Its beginning is marked by the appearance of graptolites *Parakidograptus* and *Akidograptus ascensus*. The Llandovery is subdivided into the Rhuddanian, the Aeronian, and the Telychian stages. At the close of the Telychian, the appearance of *Cyrtograptus centrifugus* marks the start of the Wenlockian era of the Silurian.

The Wenlock period is named for the Wenlock Edge in Shropshire, England. Fossils are found in siltstone and mudstone under limestone. Strangely missing from the Wenlockian fossil record is the conodont *Pterospathodus amorphognathoides*, present in earlier strata. The Wenlockian provides excellent preservations of brachiopods, corals, trilobites, clams, bryozoans, and crinoids. The era is subdivided into the Sheinwoodian and Homerian stages.

The Ludlow period, containing the important Gorstian era, is also named for a town in Shropshire. Ludlow's fossils are found in siltstone and limestone as well and is marked by the appearance of *Neodiversograptus nilssoni*. The era provides a wide display of shelled fossils.

The final portion of the Silurian is the Pridoli, the shortest epoch of the age. It is named for a nature reserve near the Prague suburb of Slivenec in the Czech Republic. The Pridolian is rich in cephalopods and bivalves. It is marked by the appearance of *Monograptus parultimus* and two new species of Chitinozoans (marine planktons) *Urnochitina* and *Fungochitina kosovensis*.

---

[3] Britannica.com

[4] Britannica.com

[5] Britannica.com

[6] Nelsonrmc, The Silurian Era – www.nelsonrmc.org/Silurian-era.htm

In North America, other names are occasionally used. The Alexandrian equates to the early Llandovery, and Ontarian to the late Llandovery. The Tonawanda period is the same as the early Wenlock, and the Lockpartian corresponds to the late Wenlock. The late Ludlow is referred to as the Cayugan based on North American regions.

For most of the span of the Silurian, life was restricted to the sea, and "there was no shortage of life in the Silurian"[7] age before the coming of amphibians, dinosaurs, mammals, and birds. However, the skies were empty, and "the deserts and valleys were choked with sand and gravel."[8]

The Silurian climate stabilized relative to the Ordovician. No longer were there so many sudden changes at the global level. The Ordovician transition ushered in a generally warmer climate, and glaciers at the South Pole began to melt. This caused a rise in the sea level. Despite its stability, frequent storms still raged across the waters and land. In time, temperatures began to drop again, cooling the environment, although not enough to restore ice age conditions.

By the end of the Silurian, the climate was more humid and warmer with a significant degree of precipitation. Coral reefs thrived in the clear sunny skies of the Southern Arid Belt across North America and northern Europe. Lingering glacial action continued near the South Pole, but for the most part, the planet went through "an unprecedented case of global warming, lifting the shackles off of evolution."[9] Oxygen levels rose steadily thanks to the continued spread of photosynthetic organisms, to the extent that oxygen levels were approximately 14%, about 30% less than today. The average global temperature of the Silurian was three degrees Celsius higher than in the present day.

In the Silurian, continental highlands were at a much lower height than in previous ages. Even though the sea level was rising, there was a place where land was rising as well. Mountain-building occurred at a rapid rate as continental plates collided. Seas moved away from the coasts or evaporated from shallow zones and plants that had lived in coastal waters were forced to live on land or die."[10]

From the late Ordovician through the Silurian and into the Devonian, the supercontinent Gondwana lost a piece called Avalonia, which broke off and drifted to the north. During that period, "three north continents collided"[11] to form a new supercontinent, Euramerica. Gondwana was a vast supercontinent centered over the South Pole that included pieces of Australia, Antarctica, India, Arabia, Africa, South America, and smaller pieces of Florida, southern Europe, Turkey, Iran, Afghanistan, Tibet, and the Malay Peninsula.

---

[7] Silurian.com, Life in the Silurian Period – www.silurian.com/geo

[8] Silurian.com

[9] Earthly Universe, Silurian Earth – First Breath of Air, Dec. 9, 2016 – www.earthlyuniverse.com/silurian-earth-first-breath-of-air/

[10] Vedantu, Silurian Period Climate – www.vedantu.com/geography/silurian-period

[11] Live Science, Silurian Period Facts: Climate, Animals & Plants – www.livescience.com43514-silurian-period.html

During the Wenlock period, India, Tibet, the Malay Peninsula and Australia were at either tropical or subtropical latitudes. A zonally uniformed climate in the north was present due to the dominance of the North Pole Ocean. The South Pole, on the other hand, was dominated by an interaction of cellular air masses over the land and water, with wide temperature variations due to summer heating and winter cooling. A high-pressure cell over the polar ocean caused the flooding of the Gondwana shelf, with a circumference of at least 28,000 kilometers. This included a belt of "persistent"[12] westerly winds that caused a boost in biological productivity. Organisms died and sank to the bottom layer of water, causing low levels of dissolved oxygen, and the development of "black shales."[13]

Tectonic activity in preparation for the Silurian Age resulted in a major mountain-building event called the *Caledonian orogeny*. The hills and mountains of Scotland and Ireland, Wales, and the northern Appalachians were formed, as were many of the mountains of Sweden and Norway. Much of North America was a shallow ocean, which enabled sunlight to penetrate, and marine animals underwent "rapid differentiation."[14] Extensive coral reefs were built from tabulate and horn coral with calcium carbonate skeleton structures.

A vast Panthalassic Ocean covered the northern polar regions, and a ring of at least six continents spanned the equator and middle latitudes. The magnetic field leaves its signature on volcanic rock. Rock that is being magnetized, cooled, or otherwise "lithified"[15] lines up its component crystals with Earth's magnetic field. These signatures are retained.

Extensive continental flooding with shallow seas formed, with a depth of a few feet to 330 feet. Some species were distributed globally for the first time, and this allowed geologists and stratigraphers to correlate layers of rock found on several continents. Much of North America, Greenland, present-day Ireland, Scotland and the Chukotski Peninsula in northern Russia belonged to the paleocontinent Laurentia. Baltica, another such continent, was separated from Laurentia by the narrow north-south Iapetus Ocean during the Wenlock period in the middle Silurian.

The geological features of the Silurian are responsible for "a wealth of natural beauty"[16] in today's time. The Niagara Falls Escarpment is a "curved ridge of resistant Silurian dolomite stretching more than 1,000 kilometers from Niagara Falls to Wisconsin's Door Peninsula and beyond. It stands up to 400 feet above the Great Lakes. In Ontario, the escarpment "fringes the eastern and northern sides of Lake Huron, and is recognized by the United National Educational, Scientific & Cultural Organization (UNESCO) as a biosphere reserve. With a "continuous footpath"[17] that follows it for 500 miles from Queenstown Heights, Ontario, to the tip of Bruce

---

[12] Britannica.com

[13] Britannica.com

[14] Live Science

[15] Britannica.com

[16] Britannica.com

Peninsula at Tobermory, in Ontario. In Iowa, Indiana, and Gotland, Sweden, the structures are called "klintar,"[18] mound reefs that reach the surface. Some of Norway's island fjords such as Tyrifjorden are lined by Silurian shales, limestones and marls.

The escarpment of Niagara Falls specifically refers to the limestone outcropping that appears in Wisconsin and other midwestern states nearly 400 million years ago. Over time, layers of sediment built up into a layer of limestone in the shallow sea and included the calcium shells of the Silurian life. Later, magnesium replaced some of the calcium, converting the limestone into "dolomitic limestone," also called *dolomite*. It is significantly harder than regular limestone.

Before the Silurian time, the Appalachian Mountains were uplifted during the Ordovician, then gradually eroded away. The transition to the Silurian was not as clearly marked in the U.S. Large reefs of the Silurian Age are found all over the American Midwest. Niagara was formed by a "dramatic erosion"[19] by the Niagara River of hard dolomitic limestone. It underlies the softer rocks of the Ordovician overlain by the Silurian limestone that was chemically converted to dolomite by the harder material, forming the hard cap of the falls.

The Wisconsin reef limestone contains no less than 191 different species of fossil life. In New York, some of the limestone contains many *eurypterids* from shallow lagoons behind the reefs. Ohio and Michigan formed vast salt deposits from inflowing sea water into "large evaporational basins."[20]

The U.S. was very near the equator during the Silurian Age. Alaska contains many stromatolite reefs (the earliest reef-building creatures before familiar corals took over). Widely exposed sandstone that stretches all the way from Alabama to New York also dates to the Silurian Age.

The Dingle Peninsula of Ireland is an excellent place to see the evidence of a major transition between two major geological divisions. Here, a marine environment transformed to a terrestrial one due to sea level fluctuations. The Silurian Dunquin Group of rocks lie next to the "reddish, purplish, greenish sandstone strata of the Silurian/Devonian Dingle Group."[21] Over 485 million years ago, Ireland was situated south of the equator. Today's landscape is due to Ordovician glaciers that melted in the Silurian during the Wenlock to Ludlow subdivisions. The Dingle Group were created by a combination of rapid sea level change to a shallow marine environment and vulcanism, "controlled by volcano-tectonic events."[22] The result is a Silurian swath 50 kilometers in length and never more than 24 kilometers in width.

---

[17] Britannica.com

[18] Britannica.com

[19] Silurian.org, 2010, The Year of the Niagara Escarpment – www.silurian.org/niagara

[20] Silurian.com, Geology, U.S.A., the Silurian in the U.S.A. – www.silurian.com/geology/usa-htm

[21] Jessica's Nature Blog, Rocks at Dunquin on the Dingle Peninsula, February 16, 2007 – www.natureinfocus.blog/2017/02/16/rocks-at-dunquin-on-the-dingle-peninsula

[22] Brian Williams, The Dingle Peninsula: A Kerry Diamond, Geo/ExPro, Vol. 17 No. 2, 2020

The Silurian features of Australia's Kalbarri National Park features red and white-banded gorges exposed at great lengths. The most notable geological feature is Tumblagooda Sandstone deposited over the Ordovician and Silurian Ages. The gorges are seen near the town of Kalbarri on the lower end of the Murchison River and coastal areas. They reach a thickness of 1,300-1,500 meters.

Kalbarri is difficult to date and was once thought to be far younger. It is a "sedimentary succession with no volcanic layers."[23] Uranium-thorium dating may prove more specific. The Tumblagooda Sandstone has undergone little tectonic activity. The deep gorges reveal massive cliff sections. The park is 186,000 hectares in area, 207 feet above sea level, and approximately 80 kilometers from the ocean.

The Dniester River is the second longest in Ukraine, originating on the slopes of Mount Rozluch in the Carpathian Mountains. Enormous Silurian deposits have been found in the western Ukrainian portion, and much data has been collected on paleomagnetic rock, including limestone and dolomite. A nearly complete Silurian sequence is present from the Llandovery to Pridoli and fossils show source origination in the Rheic Ocean.

The Silurian outcroppings in Podolia of southwestern Ukraine expose sedimentary rocks deposited on the southwest shelf of the Baltica in a basin stretching from Sweden to Moldova. On steep escarpments of the Dniester, the Silurian deposits are 900 meters in thickness and rich in fossils. Scientists have determined that the influence of geochemical change is minimal, but that the region was moved by a "regional tectonic regime and eustatic sea-level fluctuations."[24] Many fossilized examples of early jawed fish from the Silurian were unearthed there.

The Tabuk Formation of Saudi Arabia is another distinct example of Silurian features. The deposits in the Qalibah Group, the Qusaiba, and the Sharawra formations differ somewhat. The Qusaiba are dark-gray claystones and siltstones. They sit atop Ordovician and early Silurian rock deposits. Most of the Arabian features are tectonic influenced and represent a "unique layer of carbonate concretions…dated to the early Aeonian."[25] The Qusaiba sequence is the most prolific Paleozoic rock source in Saudi Arabia.

Silurian deposits in Tabuk show signs of severe thinning, an erosional feature of tectonic movement. The Ordovician/Silurian boundary within the Tabuk Formation was discovered in 1954 by R.A. Bramkamp. They were deposited in place by shallow water on a gently sloping continental shelf. The "intertidal deposition"[26] seems to be widespread. It is all part of the "Arabian Shield,"[27] a vast Pre-Cambrian complex of igneous and metamorphic rocks that

---

[23] Kalbarri National Park, Australia's Coral Coast – www.australiascoralcoast.com/destination/Kalbarri-national-park

[24] Ryszard Wrona, Academia, Silurian Succession in Podolia – www.academia.edu/54188081/silurian-succession-in-podolia-field-trip-guide-GeoShale-2012

[25] Pubs.usgs.gov, Geology of the Arabian Peninsula – www.pubs.usgs.gov/pp/0560d/report.pdf

[26] Pubs.usgs.gov

occupies one third of the entire peninsula.

The Tabuk Formation includes "vast stretches of desert"[28] in which enormous reserves of petroleum and natural gas can be found within the Silurian strata. Saudi Arabia contains 74% of the Silurian rock, and the Qalibah Formation has a subsurface thickness of 955 meters. It is a source of low-sulfur, high-gravity oil.

A significant amount of Silurian salt is mined as well, also magnesium substituted for calcium, limestone, and dolomites. In the Spiti Valley of India's Himalayan region, Silurian limestone and quartzite make up the Muth Formation at an elevation of 6,000 meters (19,700 feet).

Dating sequences taken from supercontinents indicate that at least three "highstands"[29] occurred during the Silurian Age. These occur when the sea level lies above the continental shelf. This "stimulated widespread evaporite deposition around much of Gondwana."[30] Chief among the sedentary deposits was limestone, forming continuous layers of accumulative limestone deposits when in warm water. The sea level fluctuations that brought about the "highstands" rose and fell at intervals of approximately 2.5 million years.

Similarly, late in the Silurian Age, several "lowstands"[31] downgraded the ocean's ability to circulate. The evaporations left deposits 200 to 300 meters thick. This also occurred at the Rytteraker Formation in Southern Norway, the Xiangshuyuan Formation in South China, and at the Hume Limestone of New South Wales, Australia. Through all this time, landmasses came together, and North America, central and northern Europe, and Western Europe all moved into proximity with one another.

Evaporites such as salt, anhydrite, and gypsum, "chemical precipitates"[32] accumulated in layers through the evaporation of marine waters in shallows bays and shale fields. Wedge-shaped deposits also appeared on the "continental platform margins."[33] One example in the Yukon features a layer of 1,640 feet of deep strata. In the Aberystwyth Grits Formation of Wales, the depth reaches 4,900 feet.

Sandstones and shales rest directly on Ordovician tillites, sedimentary rock in consolidated masses of unweathered blocks. Glacial till is often found as well (unsorted and unstratified rock material deposited by glacial ice). A large variation is present in tillite size, from fine powder to clasts of several meter diameters.

---

[27] Pubs.usgs.gov

[28] Britannica.com

[29] Britannica.com

[30] Britannica.com

[31] Britannica.com

[32] Britannica.com

[33] Britannica.com

Similar soil types found in Silurian deposits include "moraines," of a widely varying grain size deposited under and around glacial ice. "Loess" is best described as "fine windblown silt"[34] eroded from glaciers. "Varves" are made up of a "laminated sediment,"[35] sometimes graded and at times in an annual deposition cycle.

Despite the relatively low occurrences of vulcanism in the Silurian, it was not absent. Volcanic rocks and their "ash beds" can be found in Shropshire, England. The Laidlaw volcanoes of Canberra, Australia represent the worst vulcanism of the age.

Life

Among the most striking features of the Silurian Age, besides harboring the first creature to emerge from the water and strike out on the land, was the development of early fishes. These early creatures came with and without jaws. The first extant vertebrates, or *gnathostomes*, fall into two major monophyletic groups, *chondrichthyans* (cartilaginous fishes) and *osteichthyans* (bony fishes and tetrapods).

Scientists' understanding of the sizes of Silurian fishes has recently been altered by a find in Yunnan, China. A fossil was discovered there of a predatory *osteichthyan* almost twice the size of anything previously unearthed. The *placoderm* has been named *Megamastax amblyodus,* and it hails from the Silurian Kuanti Formation. Its length is a full meter and multiple rows of closely packed teeth can be found on the marginal jaw bones. Widely spaced pairs of blunt teeth are fused to each of the four coronoids. The mandible and maxilla have a cosmine surface with numerous spores. "Cosmine" refers to bony material of a spongy nature made of dentine layers.

---

[34] Science Direct, Soils of Antarctica – www.sciencedirect.com/topics/earth-and-planetary-sciences/tellite

[35] Science Direct

Brian Choo's picture of a restoration of *Megamastax*

A class of extinct armored prehistoric fish, the *Placodermi* represents the earliest branch of the *gnathostome* family tree, and the earliest class of jawed fishes. With a heavy bone on his head and neck, he also possesses an unusual joint in the dorsal armor between the head and neck regions. This seems to have allowed him to move his head upward as the jaw dropped down to create a larger gape.

The *Placodermi's* body was naked, except in a few cases of small scales. Unlike other jawed vertebrates, he never had teeth and did not descend from any toothed ancestors. The bony plates associated with his jaws performed the same function as teeth with razor sharp, literally "self-sharpening"[36] jaws.

---

[36] ucmp.berkeley, Introduction to the Placodermi, extinct armored fishes with jaws –
   www.ucmp.berkeley.edu/veertebrates/basa;fish.placodermi.html

It is possible that the *Placodermi* had color vision, and its evolutionary history can be compared to a brilliant light bulb that suddenly burned out, and yet in some form or other, they survived for 400 million years. They represents an "early experiment"[37] in jawed fish. Through the eons, it radiated into a large number of body shapes and "ecological niches."[38] The earliest *placoderms* were found in China in the latter part of the Early Silurian Age.

The two largest species of *placoderms* include the surprisingly massive *Dunkleosteus*, a marine predator member of *Arthrodira*. By the advent of the Devonian period, he had reached a length of 20 feet. His skull was 1.3 meters across at its widest point. Not only was he a predator, but prone to attacking his own kind.

The smaller *placoderm*, the *Bothriolepis*, had an armored head only four inches across. "Paddles"[39] on each side of its "boxy, armored body"[40] are pectoral fins, and it inhabited freshwater and marine environments (lagoons, rivers, deltas, coastal areas). *Bothriolepis* fed on invertebrates such as crustaceans and mollusks.

Other *placoderms* included a flattened sting-ray form *(rhenanids)* and those with long spines, slender, streamlined bodies, and crushing tooth plates *(ptyctodontids)*.

Chondrichthyan fishes with cartilaginous skeletons remained in freshwater environments, before invading the sea, likely because of the hot Devonian climate. Contrary to some thinking, the cartilaginous skeleton is not considered an evolutionary advance, and is "more likely degenerate rather than primitive."[41] Their precursors were probably the *petalichthyids*, sharklike *placoderms* with ossified skeletons and well-developed fins.

The evolutionary history of the *osteichthyans* extends back to the Ludlow epoch, although it is only documented by sparse and fragmentary fossils. The stem group of the bony vertebrates (clade *Euteleostomi*, is infraphylum *Gnathostomata*). *Euteleostomi* is traditionally distinguished from bony fish and are rather applied to a sister clade of *chondrichthyans*.

The prerequisites for being classified as a bony fish include a skeleton at least partly made of true bone, and flattened body scales. There must be a dermal skull roof and gular plates (bone plates that extend forward from the gill covers over part of the throat and lower jaw). The teeth must be ankylosed (with roots permanently connected to the jaw). Teeth-bearing bones must exist in the upper and lower jaws, and spines must be absent from the anal and paired fins areas.

Few *osteichthyan* fossils have been found to date, and the stem includes a "ghost lineage."[42]

---

[37] ucmp.berkeley

[38] ucmp.berkeley

[39] ucmp.berkeley

[40] ucmp.berkeley

[41] Britannica.com

[42] Evofossil, Osteichthyan Stem Group – www.evofossil.com/osteichthyan-stem-group.html

The oldest stem group is older than the stem group for *Osteichthyes* of the late Silurian. The two groups must have appeared at the same time. Thus, the *osteichthyan* stem group must also have begun in the early Silurian.

Bony fish appeared in the Silurian around 418 million years ago. Stem examples of the two groups are largely unknown. Two extinct Paleozoic groups, *acanthodians* and *placoderms* may fall into these stem groups, but their relationships and monophyletic status are both debated. Forms of *Osteichthyes* in the late Silurian include *Andreolepis hedei* and *Lophosteus superbus*. The organization of their tooth-like denticles is different from the large conical teeth of crown-group *osteichthyans*. *Andreolepis* and *Lophosteus* are certainly the oldest.

Acanthodians were the first jawed fish. They were small and shark-like in appearance. Among their notable features were large mouths and eyes. This probably meant that they preyed on smaller fish. Some had teeth in the lower jaw, while others had none at all. Dermal spines were placed at the front of all fins except the caudal.

Acanthodii is actually derived from the Greek word for "spine." They possessed growing scales that resembled the folded-in style of an onion. They had streamlined bodies, which made them fast swimmers. Although they are not the first vertebrates in history, they are "the earliest whole vertebrates to be represented in the fossil record."[43]

Andreolepis hedei is an extinct prehistoric fish, and the earliest known *Actinopterygian*, around 420 million years ago. Ray-finned fish from the late Silurian, they inhabited Russia, Sweden, Estonia, and Latvia. It was capable of shedding its teeth by basal absorption, a "primitive mode of tooth replacement."[44]

Actinopterygii are living ray-fin fishes from the family *Leptolepididae*. They arrived at the Devonian with the caudal fin and skeleton fully developed. However, they first appeared 530 million years ago, being discovered first in the Silurian. They represent a class of bony fish, a dominant group of vertebrates with 27,000 species alive today. They hail from northern Eurasia.

Actinopterygii are considered transitional while in the Silurian because they possess traits from older, more primitive groups, and of two branches of bony fish. The Guiya is considered the oldest bony fish, and the most basal of both the *Osteichthyes* and *Actinopterygii*.

Dialipina is among the most basal *osteichthyans*, sharing traits with *Actinopterygii*. *Mee mareniaeos*, a basal *osteichthyan*, shares traits with both *Actinopterygii* (the skull) and *sarcopterygians* (scales with cosmine-like structure).

Actinopterygians are the most successful vertebrates in history. Today, they enjoy the greatest

---

[43] Facweb.Furman University, The Silurian: Acanthodians – www.facweb.furman.edu/~wworthen/bio440/evolweb/silurian/acanthodian.htm
[44] Nature, The Stem Osteichthyan Andreolepis and the Origin of Tooth Replacement – www.nature.com/articles/nature19812/

number of extant species, and individuals. They dominate 99% of present-day species in both marine and freshwater environments. The lobe-finned fishes, their poor cousins *(Sarcopterygii)* constitute a minor group of fish, but "land vertebrates are their descendants."[45]

A difference between the *Actinopterygii* is that the muscles moving the fins are installed within the body wall, not as part of the fin skeleton. They move as a unit. The *Actinopterygii* are comprised of two major groups, the *chondrosteans* and the *neopterygians*. The *chondrosteans* are the most primitive, with internal skulls that resemble primitive sharks. The *neopterygians* are divided into two groups as well: primitive *neopterygians* and *teleosts*.

One of a handful of a probable *osteichthyan* stem group, *Lophosteus superbus* is a central figure in the fossil record. Discovered in the nineteenth century in Estonia, it is known for a wealth of "disarticulated scales,"[46] fin spines, and bone fragments.

Lophosteus superbus comes from the Pridoli epoch of the Silurian. His "inner dental arcade consists of numerous identical 'tooth cushions.'"[47] The skull roof includes placoderm-like elements such as rostral and central plates, along with several smaller bones. The braincase appears to have only perichondrial ossification. A dermal pelvic girdle is present. All *odontodes* lack enamel.

Fishes were widely distributed, and are known from fossils of individual scales, and from "rare body forms."[48] *Thelodonti, Heterostrace, Osteostrace, and Anaspida* were in the primitive jaw class. The non-jawed fishes included *Acanthodii, Elasmobranchii,* and *Actinopterygii*.

Among vertebrates, the *Thelodonti* are the "drifters and vagabonds"[49] of Paleozoic phylospace. They are a diverse and poorly known group of jawless fish with no established family. Covered in thick scales that appear to be distributed randomly, they take on an almost "furry"[50] quality.

The body form is Protean and was generally ignored for many years by science. *Thelodonti* is "a huge clade uniting classical *thelodonts* with other fish vertebrates. Their origin is difficult to speculate upon. Scale fossils have been discovered from the late Ordovician. We suspect that they may have been "extremely basic creatures."[51]

A major group of cartilaginous fish is the *Elasmobranchii,* said to be the first jawed fish, and includes sharks and rays. They are said to be descended from bony fish in the Silurian. However,

---

[45] My Suny Orange. Actinopterygian Fish – www.sunyorange.edu/biology/resources.prehistoric-life/actinopterygian-fish.html

[46] Pubmed, Three Dimensional Paleohistology of the Scale and Median Spine Fin of Lophosteus superbus (Pander, 1856) – www.pubmed.ncbi.nih.gov/278337941

[47] Research Gate, Osteology and Morphology of the Probable Stem Group Osteichthyan Lophosteus Superbus Pander, from the Silurian of Estonia – www.researchgate.net/publication/271849447/

[48] Palaeos, Thelodonti: Overview – www.paleos.com/vertebrates/thelodonti/

[49] Palaeos.com

[50] Palaeos.com

[51] Palaeos.com

they differ from other *agnathans* (also cartilaginous). *Elasmobranchii* have jaws, nostrils, paired pectoral and pelvic fins, and teeth.

They possess five to nine pairs of gill clefts opening individually to the exterior, rigid dorsal fins, and small placoid scales. Their teeth are arranged in several series, with the upper jaw not fused with the cranium. The lower jaw is articulated with the upper. Pelvic fins in males are modified to create claspers for the transfer of sperm. They possess no swim bladder but maintain buoyancy by heavy livers saturated with oil. The storing of oil also serves as nutrition when food is scarce. The eyes have a *tapetum lucidum*, from the Latin for "bright tapestry or coverlet." It commonly refers to a layer of eye tissue found in many vertebrates. *Elasmobranchii* have been found in two groups, one that can survive in marine water, the other in freshwater.

The *Heterostraci* serves as an important lineage that includes *ostracoderm* types as *pteraspids, cyathaspids,* and *amphiaspids.* They were restricted to middle Silurian and early Devonian. *Heterostraci* is striking for its armor-plated head, made of dentine and acellular bone. The plate covers the head, pierced laterally by a pair of "common external branchial openings."[52]

An odd genus of extinct fish appeared in the late Silurian called the *Pteraspididae* that featured a large shield on its skull, with a spear point protruding from its head. It was likely an excellent swimmer thanks to stiff wing-like fins on both sides of the body. Two protrusions originate in the head and barely cover the gills. One large spine protrudes from the back, with multiple spines on the tail for defense.

Pteraspids were streamlined planktivorous predators. The name is taken from the Greek "pteron" (wing) and aspis (shield). Five families of *pteraspids* have been distinguished, the most prominent being the *Anchipteraspididae*, the *Ulutitaspis*, and the *Rhaciaspids*.

They lacked functioning jaw muscles but swam through fields of plankton sucking in large amounts of food. Heavy armor plating protected them from sea scorpions as they fed near the surface. They are agnathan vertebrates found in Europe and North America.

The entire group of *pteraspids* has armor over the head and front of the body. Delicate, finger-like parts of the plates line the edges of the mouth, suggesting that they were filter feeders, taking in plankton from the water column.

Pteropteraspdidiae often have a "strange snout or rostrum."[53] *Doryaspis* has unusually long keels growing from the back of its head shield, with leading edges armed with tooth-like spines. These may have acted as a hydrofoil, elevating the front of the body during swimming. Lacking paired fins, stability was nevertheless provided by wing-like outgrowths growing out of the back of the head shield. It possessed a long, flexible tail with hydrodynamic advantages and received

---

[52] Palaeos.com

[53] Palaeos.com

additional lift from its snout, drawn out in a "bladelike rostrum."[54] This served a dual purpose, hydrodynamic and for probing the mud sediment for small organisms.

Discovered in numerous fossil sites around the world, the Siberian-centered *Cyathaspidida heterostracans* were bottom or suspension feeders. They can be divided into two groups, the *amphiaspids* and the *cyathaspids*. All had the cephalothorax enclosed in armor from several plates and resembled heavily armored tadpoles.

The *amphiaspids*, in addition to the armor, had all their bony plates fused together. They possessed a simple slit mouth with either reduced or no eyes. According to their supposed feeding habits, they frequently buried themselves in the lower substrate.

The armor consists of a number of plates, but that is variable. In the *amphiaspids* of Siberia, the plates are "fused into a rigid box."[55] In other groups, they are broken into numerous platelets. Still others developed "extraordinary spines and other elaborations."[56] They comprise two major groups, *Pteraspidiformes* and *Cyathaspidiformes*. Other primitive forms include *Traquairaspids, Corvaspids,* and *Lepidaspis.*

The *traquairaspids*, an order of extinct *heterostracans agnathans,* emerged from the mid-Silurian. Almond or "jet paper airplane" shaped, they are somewhat ornamental with pointed wing and dorsal crests near the posterior end of the body armor. *Corvaspids* and *Lepidaspis* are similar.

Heterostraci is arguably the first widely diversified vertebrate clade, "Lords of the vertebrate domain in the northern hemisphere."[57] They radiated rapidly in a number of diverse forms, some difficult to fit in, like *Lepidaspis*, who looked like a hot dog bun with a sausage sticking out of one end.

They carried virtually no endoskeleton. Even dermal plates were made of acellular aspidine and dentine, "requiring little metabolic investment beyond the initial cost of construction."[58] *Heterostraci* developed a single common branchial opening, minimizing the surface area exposed to parasites and avoiding multiple holes in the body wall.

The symmetrical tail was standard equipment in Silurian times, but it is unknown whether *Heterostraci* had muscular control over it. It had no internal skeleton, reinforced only by a line of scales. And yet, "it was not a conspicuously flattened fish."[59] It may have been a "slow and sloppy swimmer."[60] It was not found worldwide, so was likely not a nektonic athlete. In decline

---

[54] Palaeos.com

[55] Palaeos.com

[56] Palaeos.com

[57] Palaeos.com

[58] Palaeos.com

[59] Palaeos.com

by the onset of the Devonian, *Heterostraci* was extinct by the Carboniferous.

Anaspida is another form of jawless vertebrate and is generally considered the ancestor of the lamprey. He is a small marine *agnathans* who lacked the heavy bone shield and paired fins but had a strikingly highly hypocercal tail. *Anaspida* appeared in the early Silurian. He is totally without armor, only an "array of small, weakly mineralized scales"[61] and a row of massive scutes (external bone, horny plate, or large scale) running down the back.

His scales are tile-like, made of aspidine, a three-layered substance with a laminar base, a spongy middle, and an outer layer of cancellous, or dying bone. He sports "prominent, laterally placed eyes with no sclerotic ring, with the gill opened as a row of holes along either side of the animal, with between six and 15 pairs. *Anaspida* consists of a two-part order, monogeneric *Lasaniida* (which contains genus *Lasanius* and *Birkeniida*.)

The fish is small, between 10 to 15 centimeters in length. A pair of bony spines projects from his pectoral area and stabilization is provided by small-paired fins. In feeding, he ploughs through the bottom sediment head-first, scooping up tiny food particles into a small-rounded mouth. Fossils of *Anaspida* are rare, and he is restricted to the Silurian. His fossils are mostly found in Norway and Scotland, with a sparse record of finds in eastern Canada and the Baltic Sea.

Osteostraci, also known as *cephalaspids*, meaning "head shield"[62] hailed from the Euramerican region and lasted into the Devonian. This flattened bottom-dweller sucked up food particles from the seabed with a rounded mouth on the underside of his head. He was a good swimmer. Unlike many jawless fishes, he had pierced paired pectoral front fins, and a dorsal on the back near the tail. It was a "strong epicercal (upturned) tail"[63] the upper lobe of which produced lift at the rear of the body to keep the animal's head down.

Osteostraci had an unusual horse-shoe shaped head armored with a single plate of bone. The backward protruding *cornata* or "horns"[64] were a unique feature. He had "concentrated patches of sensory organs"[65] on both sides that must have helped him sense water-borne vibrations. They could have even been electric organs, emitting vibration to assist him in navigating murky waters. His larvae were born without armor.

From the arthropod group *Merastoma* came the sea scorpion, the marine apex predator of the Silurian Age. The *Terropterus xiushanensis*, commonly known as the sea scorpion, also came under the scientific name of *Mixopteridae*. An unchallenged predator in his own environment,

---

[60] Palaeos.com

[61] Everipedia, Anaspida – ww.everipiedia.org/Anaspida

[62] Palaeos.com

[63] Palaeos.com

[64] Palaeos.com

[65] Palaeos.com

several fossils have been found in the Xiushan Formation of China. The monster lived 435 million years ago under the specific name of *eurypterids,* "an important group of mid-Paleozoic Chelicerate arthropods whose evolution and paleological significance have attracted much attention in recent years."[66]

Sea scorpions stuck around for 200 million years, with a tail spike that could be "whipped around"[67] from side to side, spearing prey caught in its claws.

Professor Bo Wang works and teaches at the Nanjing Institute of Geology and Paleontology and Center for Excellence in Life and Paleoenvironment at the Chinese Academy of Science. He notes that *Mixopterus* members are quite large, with superficially scorpion-like *eurypterids* "bearing highly specialized anterior appendages."[68]

The sea scorpion's second and especially third pair of personal limbs are enlarged and spiny. They are presumably employed in the capture of prey, and analogies can be drawn with the "catching basket formed by spiny pedipalps (a second pair of appendages attached to the cephalothorax of arachnids) of whip spiders among the arachnids."[69]

Our knowledge of this creature is limited to only four species in two genera described 80 years ago. They include *Mixopterus kiaeri* from Norway, *Mixopterus multispinosus* from New York, *Mixopterus simonsonia* from Estonia, and *Lanarkopterus dolichoschelus* from Scotland.

All these examples are Silurian in age and come exclusively from the continent of Laurussia. This constrains our knowledge of the morphological diversity, geographical distribution, and evolutionary history of the group. *Terropterus xiushanensis* represents the first *mixopterid* from the ancient supercontinent of Gondwana and is the oldest known *mixopterid.*

The species possesses a relatively large size, reaching up to three feet in length, and larger in later discoveries. He had a "particularly enlarged prosomal limb III, characterized by a unique arrangement of spines. He was the most important predator in the Silurian marine ecosystem when there were no large vertebrate competitors.

Paleographic distribution of *mixopterids* was rather limited until now, and no examples of this group have been previously discovered in Gondwana. Only 200 species have been identified, divided into 18 families. The largest arthropod species known is *Jaekelopterus rhenaniae* measures eight feet in length. Several other *eurypterids* are nearly as large.

Fossils have been found as a rule in brackish freshwater environments, but it is believed that

---

[66] Enrico de Lazaro, Sci News, Fossils of Giant Sea Scorpion Found in China, Oct. 11, 2021 – www.scie-news.com/paleontology/terropterus-xiuhanensis-10154.html

[67] Desmond Benninor Field, Sea Scorpion, Oct. 8, 2017 – www.scienceandthesea.org/program/201710/sea-scorpion

[68] Enrico de Lazaro

[69] Enrico de Lazaro

the animal first lived in shallow coastal estuaries before moving to freshwater. Only a few species were good swimmers, and they are assumed to have been "fearsome predators"[70] with large grasping pincers that entrapped early vertebrates and various shelled animals. *Terropterus xiushanensis* has a close relative in today's oceans, the horse-shoe-crab of the order *Xiphosura*.

Terropterus xiushanensis is described by author Mihai Andrei as "dog-sized,"[71] barbed limbed, with a poisonous tail "perfectly equipped to take down every creature it encountered."[72] It came in all shapes and sizes, from a few inches to the size of a human, with a large exoskeleton and "scattered nodules,"[73] and mouths surrounded with small claws. Two new examples, possibly juvenile, have been discovered at 15 and 40 inches respectively.

The *Terropterus xiushanensis* was the only organism of its kind that traversed entire oceans and are the largest arthropods to ever exist. With binocular vision providing depth perception, they were skillful hunters. The Yale – Peabody Museum "acquired the largest and most diverse collection ever assembled,"[74] over 15,000 species, one larger than a human.

To sustain the fish, the Silurian developed an ongoing source of food in the creation of numerous marine faunae. Early extinction events for nektonic (free-swimming) and pelagic (free-floating) organisms were linked to regular sea level fluctuations. For *graptolites*, ten such extinction events were noted. These tiny organisms were named for the Greek word *graptos* (written) and *lithos* (stone).

Graptolites are small animals that encase themselves in a skeleton of collagen, similar to the material in human fingernails. A colonial animal, they group together into branches (stipes), and an individual animal is called a *zooid*. The earliest *graptolites* lived on the seabed attached to boulders or formed their own upright cones rooted in the mud.

At the beginning of the Ordovician, *graptolites* became free-floating, and were among the first creatures to colonize the open sea in the upper layers. They were common wherever food could be found, especially in the upwelling of currents, although some were also deep-water specialists.

Some colonies evolved into "enormous harvesting arrays"[75] capable of living up to 20 years. Other colonies were formed into slim, short organizations or in gently curved forms which

[70] Britannica, Giant Water Scorpion – www.britannica.com/plant/Archaefructus

[71] Mihai Andrei, Dog-Sized Scorpion was King of the Sea 440 Million Years Ago, zmescience, Oct. 20, 2021 – www.zmescience.com/science/geology/sea-scorpion-silurian-20102021/

[72] Mihai Andrei

[73] Matthew Hart, Giant Scorpions Used to Roam the Deadly Seas, Nerdist, Oct. 19, 2021 – www.nerdist.com/article/giant-sea-scorpions-fossils-discovery/

[74] Yale-Peabody Museum, Eurypterids Ancient Sea Scorpions, Invertebrate Paleontology – www.peabody.yale.edu,explore/collections/invertebrate-paleontology/euryptids-sea-scorpions

[75] bgs.ac.uk, Graptolites – www.bgs.ac.uk/discovering-geology/fossils-and-geological-time/grapholites

rotated through the water as they fed. They lived in a system of interconnected tubes in cone-like compartments (the *sicula*).

Graptolites devised numerous hydrodynamic strategies. In some cases, long "nemas" evolved to retard sinking. "Hooked, spiny, and net-like forms"[76] appeared, with a high amount of drag in order to move the colony more slowly. It may be that the collective secreted gas or low-intensity fat to help the collective rise through the water. They are classified as "colonial hemichordates that secrete a protein exoskeleton commonly preserved as a carbon film in shales."[77] Despite some preferring to live on the bottom, the "free-floaters" are a good deal more cosmopolitan. The two classes appearing in the Silurian Wenlock period include the *Pristiograptus* and the *Cyrtograptus*, both pelagic.

Now extinct, the modern *pterobranchs* serve as a close relative. All were planktonic and had only one kind of theca. They may have been hermaphroditic. Having the sexual organs of males and females within one body, they could avoid self-fertilization by temporarily becoming male, then female, or neuter. No one is absolutely certain of that theory or its process.

By far, the *Graptolites* are the most common fossil found in many parts of the world, particularly Scotland and larger Britain. The British coastline is not generally conducive to "shelly" assemblages, but still abundant around the island. They can be found in Siberia, North America and Europe, and as far away as Vietnam or Saudi Arabia. The origins of the organism were found in the Cambrian Age.

The Silurian diversification of the *graptolites* came from only one or two families to survive the Ordovician glaciation after they were largely wiped out. Their colonies can be mistaken for fossilized plants. Each colony develops a number of branches, generally found in shales and clays where marine fossils are rare. Buried in sediment, they tend to remain well-preserved, although many have been eaten by other animals. Distribution has over the years been known as worldwide.

The *Monograptus parultimus* appeared as a marker to begin the Pridoli epoch of the Silurian. It represents the advent of the final stage of *graptolites* before their final extinction during the Devonian Age. Emerged in rock exposures, they were found at the entrance to the Pozary Quarries outside of southwestern Prague. They were also found in the Eldon Group near Bubs Hill, Tasmania.

The odd *acritarch* is surprisingly old. Its name means "of uncertain origins."[78] It is a small organic entity of an artificial group, a structure that is neither carbonated nor siliceous and is not soluble in acid. Anything fitting that description must be classified as an acritarch. Remains have

---

[76] bgs.ac.uk

[77] Britannica.com

[78] Fossil, Acritarchs – www.Fossil.fandom.com/wiki/acritarcs

been found of these unicellular organisms, especially among bacterial colonies and planktonic algae.

Acritarchs are thought to be approximately 3.2 billion years old, up to 1.63 billion. They are organic-walled, consist of a central cavity and are of undetermined "biological affinities."[79]

They may include remains of different organism, from egg cases of *Metazoans* (in which cells are differentiated for specific body functions) to "resting cysts"[80] of *algae* ancestral to the *dinoflagellates*. These are primarily unicellular organisms united by a suite of unique characteristics including flagellar insertion, pigmentation, organelles, and features of the nucleus.

The oldest are poorly understood, although they most likely relate to unicellular marine *algae*. They are found in sedimentary rocks from the present back to the Archean Age. *Acritarchs* are generally isolated from rock with the use of hydrofluoric acid. It is noted that approximately one million years ago they suddenly increased in number and developed predator defenses.

The *brachiopod* is a relatively rare animal today, living only in seawater. They were far more abundant in the Silurian Age. Made of two halves, each half has a slightly different shape. *Brachiopods* feed by filtering tiny food particles from seawater.

Most of the space inside is taken up by a special organ acting as a "water pumping and filtering device."[81] They possess little to no mobility, and most hold to the bottom by a stalk. Some Silurian *brachiopods* lacked a stalk, had a flattened shell, and rested freely on the seafloor.

Around 43 species of *brachiopods* represent the most diverse group of dwellers in Silurian reefs of Wisconsin and Illinois.

Brachiopod history of life on Earth is at least 550 million years old. Its descendants survive in today's ocean, though relatively rarely. Common fossils of the Silurian Age vary considerably in size. *Gigantoproductus*, discovered in the Devonian grew up to 30 centimeters. *Rhynchonella*, on the other hand, grow two to three centimeters across.

The *brachiopod* is one of few marine animals that belongs to its own phylum of the same name. They can occupy a variety of seabed environments, from the tropics to the cold waters of the Arctic and Antarctica. They are virtually defenseless. The shell that encloses the animal's organs serves as the only protection against predators.

Most are permanently attached to their base and are incapable of actively seeking food. A few species can attach to the soft sediment underneath while others remain unattached entirely. Opening and closing their shells allows food-bearing currents to pass through it.

---

[79] Fossil

[80] Fossil

[81] bgs.ac.uk, Brachiopods – www.bfs.ac.uk/discovering-geology/fossils-and-geologist-time/brachiopods/

The two halves are made of calcite or *chitinophosphate* (calcium phosphate plus organic matter). The pedicle (or ventral) valve is externally convex in most cases. The brachial (dorsal valve) is similar, but in some cases, extremely concave or more rarely conical. Many have their valves "hinged together typically by pairs of ventral teeth and dorsal sockets."[82] The snugly fitting "joint" between the two closed valves is called the "commissure."

The external surface may show various types of ornamentation including concentric growth lines, lamellae, and wrinkles, ribs, folds, sulci, and spines. The important organ, the lophophore, has long twisted or coiled arms and filaments. Cilia (hair-like projections) attached to the filaments beat rapidly, drawing in food-bearing water.

The current carries food particles that enter between the valves through a "lateral inhalant aperture."[83] Food is caught by the filaments on the lophophore's arms and filtered water leaves via the "median exhalant aperture."[84]

Brachiopods are characteristic of shallow marine environments. In some Paleozoic rocks, *brachiopods* make up the main rock-forming component. Influenced by water depth, salinity, oxygen levels, and static lifestyle, the distribution becomes a useful tool in deducing the position of ancient shorelines and past distribution of the land and sea.

The genus *Lingula* survived virtually unchanged from the Cambrian Age to the present. Unlike others, it lives successfully in brackish water environments, like tidal mud flats. *Lingula* uses its pedicle to move up and down in the vertical burrow in which it lives. The pedicles of *Lingula* are a delicacy in some countries and are known as "lamp shells."

Conchidium is an extinct genus of *brachiopods* from the Silurian Age, with a moderately large shell that is strongly convex, and beaks that may appear at dorsal ends of the shell. It is a valuable index fossil in the marine rocks of the Lower to Middle Silurian. Developed markings include linear ridges, and costae (ribs).

A phosphatic micro-fossil may be the most prolific fossil find worldwide in the entire Silurian search. The *conodonts* are organisms shaped like teeth, and for years, that is precisely what scientists believed they were. Once that was disproven, they were believed to be annelid worms, arthropods, mollusks, chaetognaths (marine worms) and fish, even plants.

The discovery of an "articulated animal"[85] was a significant breakthrough. From the late Cambrian Age through the Silurian to the Late Triassic, the *conodont* survived. It represents the only known hard parts of an organism distantly related to the hagfish. It is preserved as "minute,

---

[82] bgs.ac.uk

[83] bgs.ac.uk

[84] bgs.ac.uk

[85] Yon Yi Zhen, Australian Museum, What are Conodonts?, 16/07/20 – www.australiamuseum/learn/australia-over-time/fossils/what-are-conodonts/

discrete, often denticulate (having tooth-like projections)."[86]

The animal measures 0.3 to 3 centimeters at the maximum, is composed of calcium phosphate, similar to the teeth and bones in humans. The *conodont* has a preserved range of colors from translucent and colorless to light brown to an opaque black.

They are preserved in most types of marine sedimentary rocks including carbonates, shells, siltstones, and chert. At times, they are found in great numbers. Since the organism's mineral composition resists dissolution, it can be extracted from carbonate rock samples using a weak acid (10% acetic acid).

"Fused clusters and complete assemblages"[87] of *conodonts* are interpreted as feeding apparatuses. With a fossil history of 300 million years, the *conodont* is among the most successful organisms to ever brave the challenges of the ancient ocean. It lived in a wide array of habitats from tropical warmth to cold high latitudes.

These small, worm-like creatures, a few to 10 centimeters of length, had varied life modes, from benthic (bottom-feeding) to nektobenthic (near-bottom) and pelagic (open ocean-dwelling, often widespread forms). *Conodonts* once occupied most major niches in the ocean. More than 1,500 species have been identified from 50 families, with many more waiting to be discovered.

The presence of *conodont* fossils is used in the construction of oceanography, climate, and biogeology of the Paleozoic world, and on to modern mapping and mineral explorations.

Corals came into being through numerous contributors, plant and animal. Among them are the *Cystiphyllum*, an extinct group of solitary *corals* found in Silurian and Devonian marine rocks. They are horn-like in shape. The oldest *coral* reefs were built by the skeletal remains of *brachiopods* and *crinoids*, among numerous other creatures.

In North America, Illinois and Wisconsin were built in large measure by *tablature coral* and *rugose coral*. Chains of tabulate reef resembled organ pipe clumps, while *rugose coral* came in the shape of a bull's horn. Another great contributor was *stromatoporoid* assemblages. *Stromatoporoids* were comprised of an extinct group of sponges that formed a hard, compact skeleton. They lived only in seawater and created currents to pump water in and out of their bodies. The *stromatoporoid* skeleton was often quite large, and generally assumed a dome shape as a major reef constructor.

Among the largest, most completely revealed barrier reefs is the one around the island of Gotland, Sweden. Great barrier reef systems "covered a substantially greater percentage of seafloor than the reefs of any portion of global history."[88] *Corals* and *arthropods* are among the

---

[86] Yon Yi Zhen
[87] Yon Yi Zhen

many animals that evolved the farthest in the Silurian. Geologists associate the Silurian with limestone, much of it laid down in reef systems (or bioherms). The earliest formation, bacteria and single-celled plants produced the lime by extracting minerals from seawater.

Groups of animals deposited their shelly skeletons into rocks. Vast skeletal quantities formed lime muds that under heat, pressure and vast periods of time turned to limestone rock.

Reefs form as barriers in the shallows, and as "isolated pinnacles"[89] in deep water. *Stromatoporoids* built domes, and tabulate corals constructed chains in lengths of two feet. Forming stable sheets over loose material was performed by the *stromatoporoids, tabulate coral* and *byrozoans.*

The water flow over the reefs was lessened by forming branching structures over the reef surface. *Tabulate* and *rugose corals* performed this function efficiently. Great majorities of organisms (over 90%) made use of the reef structure. Their skeletal remains contribute enormously to the bulk of the reef. *Sponges, rugose, crinoids, brachiopods, cephalopods, byrozoans* were but a few.

Trilobites are an extinct group of *arthropods.* They possessed a head, thorax, and tail, and are related to present-day Isopods such as sow bugs and pill bugs. All lived in seawater, and most crawled along the seafloor. Some could swim, while others burrowed under the sediment. As they are extinct, their feeding habits are unknown. They may have been scavengers of dead organisms. Some may have been predators, grazers, or filter-feeders. At least 19 species of *trilobites* lived in the Silurian reefs of Wisconsin. As they "crawled the reef in search for food on their many feet,"[90] they used their well-developed eyes and antennae to find their way.

Crinoids were an important part of reef-building as well. Resembling underwater "tree ferns" or "sea lilies," they opened up feathery arms to catch microscopic organisms in the water. Their stems were often preserved as small columnar pieces. They make up a high percentage of reef material. Officially, they fall under the category of *echinoderms.* The "sea lily" designation is faulty, as they are animals, not plants.

Echinoderms, or *"crinoids"* came from the Greek "krinon" (lily). They are related to starfish, sea urchins, and brittle stars. Traits include tubed feet, radial symmetry, appendages formed in multiples of five, and in most cases, attachment to the sea floor. *Crinoids* are noted for their feathery-like appendages that open like a flower to capture particles such as plankton. They first appeared in the Ordovician and survived the later Permian extinction, diversifying into hundreds of modern-day species.

---

[88] Silurian.com, Silurian Reefs – www.Silurian.com.geology/reefs.htm

[89] Silurian.com

[90] Meteorologiaenred, Silurian Fauna – www.Meteorologiaenred.com/en/silurian-fauna-.html

Their "pentaradial"[91] (five-fold symmetry) configuration is unusual among Silurian creatures. The largest fossil ever found is 130 feet in length, and they comprise some of Earth's earliest animals. Today fossilized elements are used for necklace beads and rosaries.

One earlier ancestor of the *crinoid* may have emerged in the Cambrian Shale called *Echmatocrinus,* originating 500 million years ago. More than 600 species of *crinoids* exist today, but more than 6,000 have lived on Earth.

It is theorized that *crinoids* came out of *blastozoans* and *cystoids*, simple but fully functional echinoderms from the early Cambrian with stalks and arms. Group *Gogiida* is often referenced by its vase-shaped body. *Blastoids* have a flower bud-shaped compartment that holds the vital organs called the theca, rather than a calyx ("husk" or "pod").

Another hypothesis is that the *crinoid* evolved from *edrioasteroids* emerged as early as the Ediacaran 635 million years ago. These organisms had a theca and five arms, radial symmetry, and calcareous plates. The Ordovician was the first period that crinoids experienced "adaptive radiation." They were to become the most diverse organism in the Paleozoic.

Some *crinoids* in the modern age do not attach to the seafloor, swimming freely. They are best described as an "upside-down starfish with a stem."[92] Stalked *crinoids* have been observed moving, but not on ocean currents. They are capable of locomotion at about two feet per hour.

The stem is made of disc-shaped pieces of endoskeleton stacked on each other, and hollow in the middle. It is held together by ligaments that decompose rapidly after death. The hollow shapes inside of discs include elliptical, circular, pentagonal, and star shaped. The column discs that are square-shaped have five holes in each.

The stem is made up of a biomineral complex of calcium bicarbonate in a sponge-like microstructure called the stereon in the embryo. It is produced by mesenchymal (can be transformed into one another) cells. Special appendages emerging from the bottom of the calyx or along the stem are not used for feeding, but as a type of "holdfast" called cirri.

Different characteristics act as a hook or can wrap itself around an object. Another type is a button-like place on the bottom of the stem that can strongly adhere to substrate such as coral. Arms, or brachials of *crinoids* splay open for feeding. Five arms are present on most fossil finds, but more are possible in modern varieties. Small ossicles are found to form the structure of the arms. They have tubular feet and cilia moving food along with the ambulacral canal of each arm.

From each canal, food transported by cilia enter into the mouth where the calyx, a "cup-shaped body"[93] containing the digestive and reproductive organs. The five-sided calcareous plates create

---

[91] Fossilera, About Crinoids – www.fossilera.com/pages/about-crinoids
[92] Fossilera

the lower cup. The mouth is atop the dorsal cup, with the anus beside it. The tegmen (protective inner layer) is the skyward surface of the calyx.

The tubed feet are covered with a sticky mucus to capture particles. Once captured, the feet move particles into the ambulacral groove and cilia moves the mucus and particle to the mouth. There is no stomach directly from the mouth, then to a short esophagus to the intestine.

The richer the food supply, the fewer number of arms are needed. The ancient *crinoid* had five arms, but some are divided into two branches making 10 arms. The nervous system has a nerve ring around the mouth extending to each arm. Another ring is associated with the senses and a third network with a neural mass at the base of the calyx with extension to each arm and the stalk. The third network controls motor action.

Crinoids are "dioecious," male or female. There are no gonads. Canals are in some of the pinnules that break open to release sperm and eggs. Fertilized eggs hatch in the water. *Crinoids* today can reproduce every 10 to 16 months. Some can intentionally drop an arm as they mature to have the correct number corresponding to the food supply.

Bivalves began to proliferate in the mid to late Silurian. The extinct genus of *Leptodesma* was represented by a group of *pelecypods* (clams) with a distinct shell. Its oval shape was accompanied by "a sharp outgrowth to the main body of the shell."[94] A troughlike flange connected the spine. Only 15 species of bivalves lived on the Silurian reefs of the upper American Midwest, and they are not common in that setting.

"The first truly terrestrial organism were fungi."[95] The oldest was classified as *Tortotubus protuberans*, which fed on detritus (waste or debris of any sort). Decomposers such as fungi and bacteria helped stock soil with the nutrients necessary to support plant life on land. Plant life was occurring through most of the Silurian but was restricted to coastal lowlands. The remainder of the interior was barren.

Tortotubus protuberans originated in the Ordovician and spread across the globe. These fossils document a manner of foraging that is highly distinct. Once finding a source of food, it produced a secondary branch that grew back down the original filament and covered itself with an envelope. These served as pipes to pass along nutrients.

The genus *Ornatifilum*, tubes of short length with an ornamented, granular surface may be the oldest example of ancient fungus as a subclass of *Tortubus*. Its affinities are restricted to *red algae* and *fungus*. Both lichen and moss were active in the mid-Silurian, but they are not the same.

---

[93] Fossilera

[94] Britannica.com

[95] Britannica.com

The two often grow in proximity to one another, on the same tree or on the same rock. Both are considered non-vascular plants, but only mosses are considered true plants. Lichen are not plants at all, rather "complex organisms formed by a symbiotic relationship between a *fungus* and an *algae* or *cyanobacteria*."[96]

Moss will have stems and leaves, where lichens will not. Mosses are among the most primitive plants on Earth, the ancestor of trees, flowers, or ferns. They have no roots, and do not produce flowers. They reproduce via spores rather than seeds and have a shallow root-like structure called a rhizoid.

Mosses cannot transport water and are vulnerable to drying up. Lichens can survive in a variety of habitats. In the absence of water, they will allow themselves to dry up and go dormant in a brittle state until water becomes available again.

Only mosses undergo photosynthesis "directly,"[97] as they contain chlorophyll, a necessary element for the process. However, *algae* and *bacteria* do photosynthesize. The *fungus* affords them protection from harsher conditions that they could not ordinarily survive. Both absorb carbon dioxide, and lichens are valuable for detoxification purposes, the sign of a healthy ecosystem.

The earliest flora of *bryophyte*-like plants appears to be cosmopolitan and once prolific and dominated the planet relatively unchanged for 30 million years. They are represented by "fossilized dispersed *cryptospores* and fragmentary plant remains."[98]

Plants are predominantly photosynthetic eukaryotes of the kingdom *Plantae*. Historically, the plant kingdom encompasses all things that were not animals, including *algae* and *fungi*. They are mostly multicellular organisms. The Silurian pre-dated many of these requirements, but among early evolutionary breakthroughs, the arrival of the rigid stalk was profound.

Simple vascular plants emerged on land with the aid of moss forests along waterways such as streambeds and lakeshores. The Silurian was the first age with fossils of extensive non-microscopic life on land. Lichens were probably the first indirect photosynthetic organisms to cling to rocky coasts of the early continents. When organic matter from decaying lichen joined the action of erosion to wear away rock, the first real soil began to build up in the shallow, protected estuaries. *Bryophytes,* such as moss, hornworts, and liverworts first appear in the late Ordovician.

The first plants were small, approximately 2.4 inches high with smooth, simply branched stems

---

[96] Forest Service District Will County, The Buzz, What's the Difference: Lichen vs. Moss/1/4/2020 –
www.reconnectwithnature.org/news/events/the-buzz/what-the-difference-lichen-vs-masses
[97] Forest Service District Will County
[98] Science, Origin and Radiation of the Earliest Vascular Land Plants – www.Science.org/doi/10.1126/science1169659

and spore sacs at the tips. Of particular note was the earliest known genus to appear. *Cooksonia* was found in the Ludlow times of the Silurian Age in Victoria, Australia.

Cooksonia is a genus of extinct plants belonging to the class of *Rhyniopsida*. It was formed by a series of "naked photosynthetic aerial axes."[99] Aerial stems formed from the inside out by an epidermis with a cuticle, a parenchymal cortex, and a nucleus with simple tracheid (a water conducting cell in xylem which lacks a perforated cell wall). Structures similar to a stomata have also been found in the cuticle, but these are absent in older examples.

Early on, *Cooksonia* exchanged water and gases directly between its cells and the external environment. The *sporangia* featured a variety of shapes, from hemispherical to spherical, and at times kidney shaped. This organism is made of several layers of sterile tissue.

Cooksonia was found in literally all sections of the world, but primarily in Ireland, Wales, England, Britain, the U.S., and Bolivia. It never grew over 10 centimeters in height but was one of the first plants ever to inhabit the Earth. It had no leaves or roots as we know them and was anchored to the ground by a "horizontal rhizome."[100]

Cooksonia emerged from the Pridoli portion of the Silurian. Adaptation to land living likely took tens of millions of years. A stem covered with spiny projection forms does not have all the features required for a vascular system. The earliest vascular plants were of the class *rhyniophytes,* slender, dichotomously branched plants without leaves or roots. The vascular system was extraordinarily simple, only water-conducting xylem.

The evolution of trees in the mid to late Silurian brought about organisms reaching no more than a few feet. However, a giant tree trunk 24 feet in height and nine feet in width discovered from the time baffled scientists for years, and the debate is not finished. Every conceivable test has been run on the fossilized remains, with some claiming the creature to be a lichen, while others believed that it was an *alga*, a plant, or something entirely different.

A general consensus has been reached that the organism that towered over all else in the Silurian Age was a giant *fungus*. 400 million years ago, plants had barely begun to colonize the land, and terrestrial plants consisted of barely anything more than stems. Roots and leaves were in their first stages of evolution. Suddenly, there was the presence of a *fungus* called *Prototaxites* in the fossil record in stark dimensional contrast to every other living thing.

Since plants attain their carbon dioxide from the air, they tend to have similar carbon 12 and carbon 13 isotope ratios to other plants of the same type. As animals consume other living things, carbon isotope ratios tend to be similar to what they eat. *Prototaxites* displayed a much wider-ranging isotope ratio than any known plant. It had to be a *fungus*.

---

[99] Prehistoria, fandom, Cooksonia, June 5, 2015 – www.prehistoria.fandom.com/es/wiki/Cooksonia

[100] Monica Sanchez, Jardineraon, Cooksonia, One of First Plants – www.jardineraon.com/cooksonia.html

Experts believe that the extreme height reached by *Prototaxites* may have been a "reproductive strategy"[101] to spread its spores over a wider area. *Prototaxites* were originally taken to be a conifer since the trunk resembles a modern tree trunk, but it was found in a time before such trees existed. Plant-like polymers were found in the fossils, but nutritional evidence supports heterotrophy, not commonly found in plants. The discovery points to the late Silurian to early Devonian as the largest land organism of the age.

Prototaxites may be composed of partially degraded water, wind, gravity influenced materials, or water-rolled mats of mixotrophic (capable of drawing energy from multiple sources) liverworts associated with *fungi* and *cyanobacteria*. Tests indicated that the glucose-based medium was 13 times that of liverwort, and that less than 20% of its carbon came from the atmosphere. The diagnosis continues to be difficult. Says Colin Schultz of the Smithsonian Institute, "It's evocative of a lot of different things, but it's diagnostic of nothing."[102]

The history of animal life in the Silurian Age begins with the discovery of two centipedes and an ancient spider in the rocks of Shropshire, England. They are the earliest record of terrestrial fauna for the period. The presence of predatory arthropods suggests that a functioning terrestrial ecosystem was in place by the late Silurian and that "the animal invasion occurred earlier than previously thought."[103]

The fossil of an ancient Silurian millipede, *Pneumodesmus newmani* was found among the Silurian rocks of Scotland. In 2004, a fragmentary insect was found in the Rhynie Chert of Scotland, the oldest known. New assemblages of Shropshire Silurian rocks included at least two other finds from the Ludlow Bone Bed, including *ostracodes, scolecodonts, bivalves,* and *languid brachiopods.* Among them was a land-based arachnid of 1.3 millimeters in length. It is flattened and opaque except for some reddish-brown color. The fragments came from an animal with four or more "walking legs."[104]

Other partial finds of legs, tergites, trunks, and antenniform fragments have been pieced together as belonging to two centipedes. The *myriapods* are defined as "many-legged *arthropods*," and include millipedes, centipedes, *pauropods*, and *symphylans*. The name comes from the Greek *myria* (myriad) and *pod* (foot). Around 15,000 species survive today.

Some species have less than a dozen legs, while other have hundreds. It is possible that one proto version of the *myriapod* dates back to the Cambrian. Since appearing, the form has

---

[101] Nick Garland, When Giant Mushrooms Ruled the Earth, Earth Archives – www.eartharchives.org/articles/when-giant-mushrooms-ruled-the-earth/index.html

[102] Nick Garland, When Giant Mushrooms Ruled the Earth, Earth Archives – www.eartharchives.org/articles/when-giant-mushrooms-ruled-the-earth/index.html

[103] Science, Land Animals in the Silurian: Arachnids and Myriapods from Shropshire, England – www.science.org/doi/10.1126/science.250.4981.658

[104] Research Gate, Land Animals in the Silurian: Arachnids and Myriapods from Shropshire, England, Dec. 1968 – www.researchgate.net/publication/6029299

changed little. Some subsist on dead plants, requiring enough vegetation in the original age for them to be self-sustaining. Others are primarily carnivorous.

Silurian animals and plants did not emerge easily or rapidly onto the land. First, many groups were required to regroup from a "disastrous climax"[105] near the end of the Ordovician. Not only was the previous age heavily glaciated but experienced a long stretch filled with extinction events. By the Silurian, half of all trilobites were extinct. The early Silurian was scarcely better than the Ordovician. The planet endured the end of a "global ice-house climate"[106] with great ice sheets at high latitudes. The world had "distinct north-south climatic zones,"[107] and flooding caused the formation of a nearly continuous sea from New York to Nevada, and many other areas. The mean oxygen level finally rose to an atmospheric level of 19%, with carbon dioxide levels at 4,600 parts per million. Great periods of storms raged after temperatures briefly decreased as the Silurian "began to cool the environment a bit without reaching the extremes of an ice age."[108]

From the late Ordovician to the Silurian, extinction events caused the demise of 85% of all Ordovician species, second only the late Permian-Triassic extinction, and twice as severe as the K-T extinction at the end of the Cretaceous Period that eliminated the dinosaurs. Fortunately, earth's atmosphere developed "an effective ozone layer concentration."[109] No iridium has been detected to suggest any collision with a comet or other interplanetary body.

Several smaller Silurian extinctions slowed the evolution of nektonic and pelagic organisms considerably. The demise of these organisms was tied directly to sea level changes. From 52% to 79% of planktonic animals disappeared.

Photosynthesis eventually took hold of the Silurian as a reliable sustenance of life, but not immediately or directly, entirely depending on the sea levels. Early Silurian extinctions, resulting from Ordovician events, claimed 26% of all marine invertebrate families and 60% of all marine invertebrates generally. Only 17% of all *brachiopods* survived, and 20% out of 70 *tabulate* and *heliolitid coral* genera came through the events. Out of 71 *trilobite* genera, 63% survived the Ordovician-Silurian boundary.

The brief cooling period reverted to a temperature rise in the late Silurian, entering the Devonian Age in an intense heat that saved some life forms and destroyed others.

[105] National Geographic, Silurian Period – www.nationalgeographic.com/science/article/silurian

[106] Sites, Google, Silurian Period, An Age of Land Plants and Fish Diversification –
www/sites.google.com/site/paleoplant/geological/phanezoic/paleozoic/silurian

[107] Sites, Google

[108] Meterologiaenred, Silurian Fauna – www.Meterologiaenred.com/en/silurian-fauna.html

[109] National Park Service, Silurian Period – 443.8 to 419.2 million years ago – www.nps.gov/articles/000/silurian-period.htm

Online Resources

<u>Other books about ancient history by Charles River Editors</u>

Further Reading

Andrei, Mihai, Dog-Sized Scorpion was King of the Sea 440 Million Years Ago, zmescience, Oct. 20, 2021 – www.zmescience.com/science/geology/sea-scorpion-silurian-20102021/

Benninor, Desmond, Field, Sea Scorpion, Oct. 8, 2017 – www.scieceandthesea.org/program/201710/sea-scorpion

bgs.ac.uk, Brachiopods – www.bfs.ac.uk/discovering-geology/fossils-and-geologist-time/brachiopods/

bgs.ac.uk, Graptolites – www.bgs.ac.uk/discovering-geology/fossils-and-geological-time/grapholites

Britannica, Science, Silurian Period – www.britannica.com/science/Silurian-Period

Britannica, Giant Water Scorpion – www.britannica.com/plant/Archaefructus

de Lazaro, Enrico, Sci News, Fossils of Giant Sea Scorpion Found in China, Oct. 11, 2021 – www.scie-news.com/paleontology/terropterus-xiuhanensis-10154.html

Earthly Universe, Silurian Earth – First Breath of Air, Dec. 9, 2016 – www.earthlyuniverse.com/silurian-earth-first-breath-of-air/

Encyclopedia.com, James Hall, Oxford University Press – www.encyclopedia.com/people/science-and-technology/geology-and-oceanography-biographies/james-hall

Everipedia, Silurian – www.everipedia.com/Silurian

Evofossil, Osteichthyan Stem Group – www.evofossil.com/osteichthyan-stem-group.html

Facweb.Furman University, The Silurian: Acanthodians – www.facweb.furman.edu/~wworthen/bio440/evolweb/silurian/acanthodian.htm

Forest Service District Will County, The Buzz, What's the Difference: Lichen vs. Moss/1/4/2020 –www.reconnectwithnature.org/news/events/the-buzz/what-the-difference-lichen-vs-masses

Fossil, Acritarchs – www.Fossil.fandom.com/wiki/acritarcs

Fossilera, About Crinoids – www.fossilera.com/pages/about-crinoids

Garland, Nick, When Giant Mushrooms Ruled the Earth, Earth Archives –
www.eartharchives.org/articles/when-giant-mushrooms-ruled-the-earth/index.html

Geology, Prototaxites – www.geologyin.com/2020/03

Hart, Matthew, Giant Scorpions Used to Roam the Deadly Seas, Nerdist, Oct. 19, 2021 –
www.nerdist.com/article/giant-sea-scorpions-fossils-discovery/

Jessica's Nature Blog, Rocks at Dunquin on the Dingle Peninsula, February 16, 2007 –
www.natureinfocus.blog/2017/02/16/rocks-at-dunquin-on-the-dingle-peninsula

Kalbarri National Park, Australia's Coral Coast –
www.australiascoralcoast.com/destination/Kalbarri-national-park

Live Science, Silurian Period Facts: Climate, Animals and Plants –
www.livescience.com/43514-siberian-period.html

Meteorologiaenred, Silurian Fauna – www.meteorologianred.com/en/silurian-fauna.html

My Suny Orange. Actinopterygian Fish – www.sunyorange.edu/biology/resources.prehistoric-
life/actinopterygian-fish.html

National Geographic, Silurian Period - www.nationalgeographic.com/science/article/silurian

National Park Service, Silurian Period – 4438 to 419.2mya –
www.nps.gov/articles/000/silurian-period.htm

Nature, The Stem Osteichthyan Andreolepis and the Origin of Tooth Replacement –
www.nature.com/articles/nature19812/

Nelsonrmc, The Silurian Era – www.nelsonrmc.org/Silurian-era.html

Paleontology World, Cephalaspis: Silurian-Devonian Jawless Fish were Ecologically
Diversified – www.paleontologyworld.com/exploring-prehistoric-life/cephalaspis-silurian-
devonian-jawless-fish-were-ecologically

Palaeos, Thelodonti: Overview – www.paleos.com/vertebrates/thelodonti/

Prehistoria, fandom, Cooksonia, June 5, 2015 –
www.prehistoria.fandom.com/es/wiki/Cooksonia

Pubmed, Three Dimensional Paleohistory of the Scale and Median Spine Fin of Lophosteus superbus (Pander, 1856) – www.pubmed.ncbi.nih.gov/278337941

Pubs.usgs.gov, Geology of the Arabian Peninsula – www.pubs.usgs.gov/pp/0560d/report.pdf

Research Gate, Osteology and Morphology of the Probably Stem Group Osteichthyan Lophosteus Superbus Pander, from the Silurian of Estonia www.researchgate.net/publication/271849447_Osteology_and_morphology_of_the_probable_st em_group_osteichthyan_lophosteus_superbus_Pander_from-the_Silurian_of_Estonia

\Research Gate, Land Animals in the Silurian: Arachnids and Myriapods from Shropshire, England, Dec. 1968 – www.researchgate.net/publication/6029299

Sanchez, Monica, Jardineraon, Cooksonia, One of First Plants – www.jardineraon.com/cooksonia.html

Science, Origin and Radiation of the Earliest Vascular Land Plants – www.Science.org/doi/10.1126/science1169659

Science Direct, Soils of Antarctica – www.sciencedirect.com/topics/earth-and-planetary-sciences/tellite

Silurian.com, Geology, U.S.A., the Silurian in the U.S.A. – www.silurian.com/geology/usa-htm

Silurian.com, Life in the Silurian Period – www.silurian.com/geology/life.htm

Silurian.org, 2010, The Year of the Niagara Escarpment – www.silurian.org/niagara

Sites, Google, Silurian Period, an Age of Land Plants and Fish Diversification – www.sites.google.com/www.site/paleoplant/geologic/phanerzoic/paleozoic/silurian

Ucmp.berkeley, The Silurian Period – www.ucmp.berkeley.edy/silurian.php

Ucmp.berkeley, Introduction to the Placodermi, extinct armored fishes with jaws – www.ucmp.berkeley.edu/veertebrates/basa;fish.placodermi.html

Vedantu, Silurian Period Climate – www.vedantu.com/geography/silurian-period

Williams, Brian, The Dingle Peninsula: A Kerry Diamond, Geo/ExPro, Vol. 17 No. 2, 2020 Ryszard Wrona, Academia, Silurian Succession in Podolia – www.academia.edu/54188081/silurian-succession-in-podolia-field-trip-guide-GeoShale-2012

Yale-Peabody Museum, Eurypterids Ancient Sea Scorpions, Invertebrate Paleontology –

www.peabody.yale.edu,explore/collections/invertebrate-paleontology/euryptids-sea-scorpions

Wrona, Ryszard, Academia, Silurian Succession in Podolia –
www.academia.edu/54188081/silurian-succession-in-podolia-field-trip-guide-GeoShale-2012

Zhen, Yon Yi, Australian Museum, What are Conodonts?, 16/07/20 –
www.australiamuseum/learn/australia-over-time/fossils/what-are-conodonts/